Foreword

These two talks were originally given at the West Coast school and camp held near Los Angeles, California, in September 1955. They offer a popularized account of the main line of evolution from fish to mankind, from savagery to civilization, and from Indian life to contemporary capitalism in the United States. This is an extremely simplified outline of the immense and complex range of that evolutionary process. The facts set forth are well enough known—but their interpretation here differs from that taught in the schools and universities of capitalist America.

These talks were designed as an introduction to a study of the march of mankind from the viewpoint of scientific socialism.

It is especially directed toward newly awakened minds, concerned about the fundamental problems of life in our time and seeking enlightenment on the main issues of the social and political struggle.

Its arguments are aimed against two prevailing notions which tend to reinforce antisocialist prejudices and uphold belief in the sanctity of the existing system. One is the general idea that it is impossible, undesirable or somehow unscientific to seek out the central course of development in history, above all in the history of society; to link together its successive stages and place them in proper sequence; to distinguish the lower form from the higher; and indicate the nature of the next steps.

The second prejudice is more specific, although it is supported by the first. This is the assumption that the established capitalist regime in the United States embodies the highest attainable mode of life and an unsurpassable type of social organization.

These propositions, I hope to show, are wrong in theory and thoroughly reactionary in their practical consequences. Socialist theory has the merit of explaining how and why the growing discontent with the existing setup among the working people and their strivings for a better way of life are reasonable, realistic, and founded on sound scientific premises. The instinctive drive of the workers toward a fundamental reorganization of the capitalist social and political structure accords with the main line of human progress.

These conclusions are already taken for granted in many parts of the globe which are usually regarded as backward by the American people. However, it must be said that although our country is the most modernized in many respects, from superhighways to color television, it is most backward in recognizing—and acting upon—the elementary truths of evolutionary science and revolutionary socialism.

I hope this little pamphlet will help some fellow-countrymen and women to catch up with the thinking of the more progressive sections of mankind by clearing away capitalist-fostered prejudices, which obscure the real meaning of American history and block the road to the next stage of American civilization.

October 1956

How humanity climbed to civilization

I propose first to trace the main line of human development, from our remote animal ancestors to the present, when humanity has become lord of the earth but not yet master of its own creations, not to mention its own social system. After that, I will deal with the central course of evolution in that specific segment of society that occupies the bulk of North America and represents the most developed form of capitalist society.

I will try to show not only how our national history is related to world development but also how we, collectively and individually, fit into the picture. This is a broad and bold undertaking, a sort of jet-propelled journey through the stratosphere of world history. It is forced upon us by the urge to grasp the whole vast spread of events and to understand our specific place within them, as well as by the very dynamic of scientific theory in sociology, which has its highest expression in Marxism. The movement based upon scientific socialism, which prepares most energetically for the future, likewise must probe most deeply into the past.

* * *

I shall start from the political case history of an individual. In January 1935 a book appeared which set the style for a series of reflective reports on the trends of our times. It had considerable influence upon radicalized intellectuals here until the outbreak of the Second World War. That book, *Personal History,* was written by Vincent Sheean. This autobiography was a serious effort to find out what the history of his generation was leading to and what his attitude should be toward its mainstream and its cross currents.

Sheean told how he started as an ignorant student at the University of Chicago at the close of the First World War. He knew as little about the fundamental forces at work in the world then as millions like him today who are encased in a similar provincialism. As he remarked:

> The bourgeois system insulated all its children as much as possible from a knowledge of the processes of human development, and in my case succeeded admirably in its purpose. Few Hottentots or South Sea Islanders could have been less prepared for life in the great world than I was at twenty-one.

This innocent American went abroad as a newspaperman and learned from the great events of the twenties. He observed the effects of the First World War and the Russian revolution; he witnessed the stirrings in the Near East, in Morocco and Palestine— precursors of the vaster colonial disturbances after the Second World War. He was also a spectator and played an incidental role in the defeated second Chinese revolution of 1926. His experiences were topped by the economic collapse of capitalism after 1929 and the spread of fascism in Europe.

These upheavals jolted Sheean from his doze, opened his eyes, and propelled him toward Marxism and the revolutionary socialist movement. He was swept along in the swirling torrent of that first stage in the crack-up of capitalist civilization—and began to recognize it as such. Great social, economic, and political events exposed the bankruptcy of the ideas about the world he had acquired through his middle-class education in the Midwest and impelled him to cast them off.

Sheean found in Marxism the most convincing explanation of the processes of social development and the causes of the decisive events of his own age. He was inspired by its ability to answer the question that besets every thinking person: What relation does my own life have to those who have preceded me on this earth, all my contemporaries, and the incalculable generations who will come later?

Scientific, political, and moral considerations combined to attract him to the science of the socialist movement. Sheean admired Marxism, he emphasized, because it took "the long view." This is not a phrase he coined, but one he borrowed from a participant in the struggle. Marxists, he noted, were or should be guided not by partial views and episodic considerations but by the most comprehensive outlook over the expanse of biological evolution and human achievement.

The all-embracing synthesis of history offered by Marxism contrasted sharply with the worm's-eye view he had had in the Midwest. The interior of the United States had the most up-to-date gadgets, but it was dominated by extremely old-fashioned ideas about social evolution.

Sheean had caught on to one of the outstanding features of that system of thought that bears the name of its creator, Karl Marx. Scientific socialism does provide the most consistent, many-sided, and far-reaching of all the doctrines of evolution—and revolution. "The long view" it presents is the march of mankind seen in its full scope, its current reality, and its ultimate consequences, so far as that is possible under present limitations.

*　*　*

What was this long view that attracted Vincent Sheean and so many millions before him and since? What can a review of the process of evolution, analyzed by Marxist methods, teach us about the way things change in this world?

We can single out four critical turning points in the timetable of evolution. The first was the origin of our planet about three or four billion years ago. The second was the emergence of life in the form of simple one-celled sea organisms about two and a half billion years ago. (These are only approximate but commonly accepted dates at the present time.) Third was the appearance of the first backboned animals about four to five hundred million years ago. Last was the creation of mankind, within the past million years or so.

The most revolutionary feature of the fish was the fact that it became the starting point for the entire hierarchy of backboned creatures that has culminated in ourselves.

Let us begin with the third great chapter in this historical panorama—the first fish species. The American Museum of Natural History has prepared a chart that portrays the principal stages in organic evolution from the first fish up to ourselves, the highest form of mammalian creatures. The backbone introduced by the fish was one of the basic structures for subsequent higher evolution.

Astraspis, as one of the first vertebrate specimens is called, lived in the Paleozoic era near Cannon City, Colorado, where its plates were found in delta deposits. This native American of four to five hundred million years ago was very revolutionary for its day. Here is what a popular authority, Brian Curtis, says about this development in *The Life Story of the Fish:*

> An animal with a backbone does not seem strange to us today. But at the time that the first fish appeared upon earth,

which we know from geological records to have been roughly five hundred million years ago, he must have seemed a miraculous thing. He was the very latest model in animal design, a radical, one might almost say a reckless experiment of that force which we find it convenient to personify as Mother Nature.

What did its "radicalism" consist of?

> For up to that time no creature had ever been made with the hard parts inside instead of outside. . . . Nature might be said to have had a brainstorm, abandoned all the earlier methods and turned out overnight something absolutely new and unheard of.

Although the fish retained some of the old external armor, what was decisive from the standpoint of evolution was its acquisition of the backbone. This converted the fish into a creature basically different from anything living before. Thus, the new backboned type both *grew out of* the old and *outgrew* it. But that is not all. It then went on to conquer new realms of existence and activity. The most revolutionary feature of the fish was the fact that it became the starting point for the entire hierarchy of backboned creatures that has culminated in ourselves.

These first vertebrates subsequently advanced from the fish through the amphibians (which lived both in water and on land), through the reptiles, and finally branched off into the warm-blooded creatures: birds and mammals. Mankind is the culminating point of mammalian development. This much of animal evolution is accepted by all scientific authorities.

But these ideas and facts, so commonplace today, were the subversive thoughts of yesterday. We readily adopt this scientific view of organic evolution without realizing that this very act of acceptance is part of a reversal in human thinking about the world and the creatures in it, which has taken place on a mass scale only during the past century. Recall, for example, the prevalence of the Biblical myth of creation in the Western world up to a few generations ago.

Two aspects of the facts about the vertebrates deserve special discussion. First, the transfer of the bony parts of the fish from the outside to the inside embodied a qualitatively new form of organic structure, a break in the continuity of development up to that time, a jump onto a higher level of life. Every biologist acknowledges this fact. But this fact has a more profound significance, which tells us much about the methods of evolutionary change in general. It demonstrates how, at the critical point in the accumulation of changes outside and inside an organism, the conflicting elements that compose it break up the old form of its existence, and the progressive formation passes over, by way of a leap, to a qualitatively new and historically higher state of development. This is true not only of organic species but of social formations and systems of thought as well.

This radical overturn is undeniable in the case of the birth and evolution of the fish and its ultimate surpassing by higher species. But it is much harder for many people to accept such a conclusion when it comes to the transformation of a lower social organization into a higher social organization. This reluctance to apply the teachings of evolution consistently to all things, and above all to the social system in which we live, is rooted in the determination to defend powerful but obsolete and narrow class interests against opposing forces and rival ideas that aim to create a genuinely new order of things.

The second point to be stressed is the fact that the fish, as the first vertebrate, occupies a specific place in the sequence of the evolution of organisms. It is one link in a chain of the manifestations of life extending from one-celled protozoa to the most complex organisms. This first creature with a backbone came out of and after a host of creatures which never had such a skeletal structure and in turn gave rise to superior orders which had that and much more.

Contradictory as it is, many scholars and scientists who take the order of evolution of organic species for granted, stubbornly resist the extension of the same lawfulness to the changing species of social organizations. They will not admit that there has been, or can be, any definite and discernible sequence in the social development of mankind analogous to the steps in the progress from the invertebrates to the fish, through the reptile and mammalian creatures, up to the advent of mankind.

This skepticism in sociology is especially pronounced in the present century, and in our own country and its colleges. Thinkers of this type, of course, know that there have been many changes in history, that many diverse formations are found in the fields of anthropology, archaeology, history, sociology, and politics.

What they deny is that these typical manifestations of social life can—or even should—be arranged in any determinate order of historical development in which each has its given place from the beginning to the end, from the lower to the higher. They teach that all the various forms of culture and ways of life are merely dissimilar to one another and that it is impossible or unnecessary to try to discover any regular sequence or lawful affiliation in their emergence into social reality.

This view and method is thoroughly antievolutionary, antiscientific, and essentially reactionary. But it is explainable. The denial of the possibility of finding out the order of advancement in social structures springs—if you will permit the analogy—from the resistance by today's invertebrates to the oncoming vertebrates who represent a superior form of organization and are destined to supplant them in the struggle for social survival.

The evolutionary record itself, starting with the upward climb of the fish, most effectively refutes this tenacious conservatism. The first vertebrate was followed by six further progressive types of fish in the next hundred million years. The most advanced was a freshwater, medium-sized carnivorous species whose fossils have been found in Canada. Although this specimen spent much of its life in the water, it had acquired many of the functions required for living on land. Fish, as you know, are customarily at home in water, breathe through gills, and have fins. It was unbecoming to established fish-nature for the first amphibians to get up out of the water and crawl onto land, breathe through lungs, and move about on legs.

Let us imagine a fish (if you will go along with the fancy) who looked backward rather than forward, as some fish do. This backward-looking fish could exclaim to the forward-moving amphibians: "We fish, the oldest inhabitants, have never before done such things; they can't be done; they shouldn't be done!" And, when the amphibians persisted, could shriek: "These things mustn't be done; it's subversive of the good old order to do them!" However, the resistance of inertia did not prevent some water dwellers from turning into land animals.

Animal life continued to move forward as species were modified and transmuted in response to decisive changes in their genetic constitutions and natural habitats. Amphibians turned into reptiles, which had better developed brains, were rib-breathing, egg-laying, had limbs for locomotion, and well-developed eyes. The reptile kingdom evolved gradually toward the mammal, with transitional types that had features belonging to both, until once again a full-fledged new order stepped into the world.

About 135 million years ago, the animal prototype that gave rise to our own tree-living ancestor emerged. This was a rodent-like creature who took another big leap in evolutionary adaptation and activity by quitting the land for the trees. Arboreal existence over six hundred thousand years so altered our animal ancestors from head to toe, from grasping functions to teeth changes, that they elevated themselves to monkey and ape forms. The kinship of the latter with our own kind is so close that it is difficult to distinguish an embryo of the highest apes from that of a human.

The natural conditions had at last been created for the emergence of mankind. It seems likely that changes in climate and geographical conditions connected with the first Ice Age drove certain species of primates down from the trees, out of the forests and onto the plains. A series of important anatomical developments paved the way for the making of the human race. The shortening of the pelvic bone made it possible for the primate to stand erect, to differentiate forelimbs from hindlimbs and emancipate the hands. The brain became enlarged. Binocular vision and vocal organs made human sight and speech possible.

The central biological organ for the making of mankind was the hand. The hands became opposed to the legs, and the thumb became opposed to the four fingers. This opposition between the thumb and the other fingers has been one of the most fruitful and dynamic of all the unions of opposites in the evolution of humanity. The thumb's ability to counterpose itself to each of the other fingers gave the hand exceptional powers of grasping and manipulating objects and endowed it with extreme flexibility and sensitivity. This acquisition made possible the biological combination of hand-eye-brain. Combined with the prolonged period of care by the mother for her offspring, the natural prerequisites for social life were at hand.

* * *

At this point something should be said about the most common argument against socialism: "You can't change human nature!" How much substance is there to this contention?

Once the record of organic evolution is accepted, one proposition, at least, inevitably flows from it: *Fish nature can be changed!* It has been changed into amphibian, reptile, bird, mammalian, and, ultimately, into human natures. The salt in our bodies is one reminder, among many, of our descent from great-grandfather fish in the oceans of ages ago.

This poses the following pertinent questions to the resisters to social change: If fish can change, or be changed so much, on what grounds can narrow restrictions be imposed upon the changeability of mankind? Did our species lose its plasticity, its potentialities for radical alteration somewhere along the line from the transition of the primate to the human?

The contrary is the case. In the passage to humanity, our species not only retained all the capacities for progressive change inherent in animality but multiplied them to an infinitely higher degree, lifting them onto an entirely new dimension by creating previously unknown ways and means of evolutionary progress.

The fundamentally new powers mankind acquired were the powers of production, of securing the means of sustenance through the use of tools and joint labor, and sharing the results with one another.

It required four to five hundred million years to create the biological conditions necessary for the generation of the first subhumans. This was not brought about through anyone's forethought or foresight, or in accord with any plan, or with the aim of realizing some preconceived goal. It happened, we may say, as the lawful outcome of a series of blind and accidental developments in the forms of natural life, spurred forward in the struggle for survival, which eventually culminated in the production of a special kind of primate equipped with the capacities for acquiring more than animal powers.

At this juncture, about a million or so years ago, the most radical of all the transmutations of life on this planet took place. The emergence of mankind embodied something totally different which became the root of a unique line of development. What was this? It was the passage from animal separatism to human collectivism, from purely biological modes of behavior to the use of acquired social powers.

Where did these added artificial powers come from that have marked off emerging mankind from all other animal species, elevated our species above the other primates, and made mankind into the dominant order of life? Our dominance is indisputable because we command the power to destroy ourselves and all other forms of life, not to speak of changing them.

The fundamentally new powers mankind acquired were the powers of production, of securing the means of sustenance through the use of tools and joint labor, and sharing the results with one another. I can do no more than single out four of the most important factors in this process.

The first was associated activities in getting food and dividing it. The second was the use, and later the manufacture, of implements for that purpose. The third was the development of speech and of reasoning, which arose from and was promoted by living and working together. The fourth was the use, the domestication, and the production of fire. Fire was the first natural force, the first chemical process, put to socially productive use by ascending humanity.

Thanks to these new powers, emerging mankind enormously speeded up the changes in our own species and later in the world around us. The record of history for the past million years is essentially one of the formation of humanity and its continual transformation. This in turn has promoted the transformation of the world around us.

What has enabled mankind to effect such colossal changes in himself and his environment? All the biological changes in our stock over the past million years, taken together, have not been a prominent factor in the advancement of the human species. Yet during that time humanity has taken the raw material inherited from our animal past, socialized it, humanized it, and partially, though not completely, civilized it. The axis of human development, contrasted to animality, revolves around these social rather than biological processes.

The mainspring of this progress comes from the improvement

of the powers of production, acquired along the way and expanded in accordance with man's growing needs. By discovering and utilizing the diverse properties and resources of the world around him, man has gradually added to his abilities of producing the means of life. As these have developed, all his other social powers—the power of speech, of thought, of art, and of science, etc. have been enhanced.

The decisive difference between the highest animals and ourselves is to be found in our development of the means and forces of production and destruction (two aspects of one and the same phenomenon). This accounts not only for the qualitative difference between man and the other animals but also for the specific differences between one level of human development and another. What demarcates the peoples of the Stone Age from those of the Iron Age, and savage life from civilized societies, is the difference in the total powers of production at their disposal.

What happens when two different levels of productive and destructive power measure strength was dramatically illustrated when the Spanish conquerors invaded the Western Hemisphere. The Indians were armed with bows and arrows and slings; the newcomers had muskets and gunpowder. The Indians had canoes and paddles; the Spaniards had big sailing ships. The Indians wore leather or padded jackets for protection in warfare; the Spaniards had steel armor. The Indians had no domesticated draught animals but went on foot; the Spaniards rode horses. Their superior equipment inspired terror and enabled the conquistadores to defeat their antagonists with inferior manpower.

This basic proposition of historical materialism should be easier for us to grasp because we are privileged to witness the first stage of a technological revolution comparable in importance to the taming of fire a half million years ago. That is the acquisition of control over the processes of nuclear fission and fusion. This new source of power has already revolutionized the relations among governments and the art of warfare; it is about to transform industry, agriculture, medicine, and many other departments of social activity.*

What brought this technological revolution about? Mankind underwent no biological changes in the preceding period. Nor were there any sudden alterations in human modes of thinking, in their sentiments, or their moral ideas. This incalculably powerful force of production and destruction issued from the entire previous development of society's productive forces and all the scientific knowledge and instruments connected with them. Atomic power is the latest link in the chain of acquired powers that can be traced back to the earliest elements of social production: associated labor in securing the necessities of life, tool using and making, speech, thought, and fire. Atomic energy is the latest fruit of the seeds planted back in ancient society, which have been cultivated and improved by humanity in its upward climb.

*   *   *

Let us come back to that remarkable organ of ours, the hand. The hand, which among the primates originally conveyed food to the mouth, was converted by humanity into an organ for grasping and guiding the materials used and then shaped for tools. The hand is the biological prototype of the tool and the handle; it is the prerequisite and parent of laboring activity. The passage from the hand to the tool coincides with the creation of society and the progressive development of mankind and its latent powers.

The connection between the most rudimentary tools and the complex material instruments of production in today's indus-

---

*The reader should bear in mind that these comments about nuclear power were made in 1955. Since then, the life-threatening hazards of the nuclear industry have become appallingly clear. I concur with the growing worldwide antinuclear movement that because of the dangers inherent in disposing nuclear wastes as well as in mining and processing nuclear fuels the entire nuclear industry should be dismantled.—GN, 1979

trial system has been graphically illustrated in a chart prepared for the Do-All Corporation, of Des Plaines, Illinois, sponsor of a traveling exhibit on "How Basic Tools Created Civilization." This exhibit, which claims to be "the first attempt ever made to assemble the complete history of man's tools," documents the stages in the progress of technology.

The first known tools formed by man, called eoliths, date back, some scientists say, to one and a half million years ago. These were sections of broken stone with edges useful for cutting meat, scraping hides, or digging for roots. They were little more than simple extensions of the hand. They were not designed for specific functions but were adaptable for pounding, throwing, scraping, drilling, cutting, etc.

In the next stage, tools underwent improvement along two main lines: their cutting edges were made more efficient; and they became fashioned for special purposes. Men learned to chip stone to a predetermined shape, thereby producing a sharper cutting edge. A wider variety of working tools, such as axes, sharp-pointed drills, thin-edged blades, chisels, and other forerunners of today's hand tools, came into existence.

These tools reduced the time needed to produce sustenance and shelter, thereby raising the social level of production and improving living conditions. Moreover, these new productive activities enhanced man's mental capacities. The complexity of special-purpose tools indicates the development of a mentality capable of understanding the necessity of producing the *means* before the *end* could be attained. Mental concepts of specific use preceded both the design and construction of these special-purpose tools.

Each of the subsequent steps in the improvement of tool using and tool making likewise resulted in the economizing of labor time, an increased productivity of labor, better living conditions, and the growth of man's intellectual abilities. The motive force of human history comes from the greater productivity of labor made possible by decisive advances in the techniques and tools of production.

This can be seen in the development of hunting. At first, mankind could as a rule capture only small and slow animals. Regular consumption of big game was made possible by the invention of such hunting weapons as the thrusting spear, the throwing spear, the spear-thrower, and the bow and arrow. The latter was the first device capable of storing energy for release when desired. These implements increased the range and striking force of primitive hunters and enabled them to slaughter the largest and fleetest animals.

All the basic hand tools in use today—the ax, adz, knife, drill, scraper, chisel, saw—were invented during the Stone Age. The first metal, bronze, did not replace stone as the preferred material for tool making until about 3,500 years ago. Metal not only imparted a far more efficient and durable cutting edge to tools but enabled them to be resharpened instead of thrown away after becoming dulled.

The principal epochs in the advancement of humanity can therefore be divided according to the decisive improvements effected in securing food supplies.

During the period when bronze tools were the chief implements of production, means and standards of measurements were devised; mathematics and surveying were developed; a calendar was calculated; and great advances were made in sculpturing. Such basic inventions as the potter's wheel, the balance scale, the keystone arch, sailing vessels, and glass bottles were created.

About 2,500 years ago, iron, the most durable, plentiful and cheap metal, began to displace bronze in tool making. The introduction of iron tools tremendously advanced productivity and skills in agriculture and craftsmanship. They enabled more food to be grown and better clothing and shelter to be made with less expenditure of time and energy; they gave rise to many comforts and conveniences. Iron tools made possible many of the achievements of Greece and Rome, from the Acropolis of Athens to the tunnels, bridges, sewers, and buildings of Rome.

The energy for all these earlier means and modes of production was supplied exclusively by human muscles, which, after the domestication of herds, was supplemented to some extent by animal muscle power. The Industrial Revolution of the eighteenth century was based upon the utilization of energy from other sources, from fossil fuels such as coal. The combination of mechanical power generated by steam engines, machine tools, improved implements, and production machinery, plus the increased use of iron and steel, have multiplied society's powers of production to their present point. Nowadays, machines and tools operated by mechanical and electrical power are the principal material organs of our industry and agriculture alike.

The most up-to-date machine tools have been developed out of simple hand tools. While using hand tools, men began to understand and employ the advantages of the lever, the pulley, the inclined plane, the wheel and axle, and the screw to multiply their strength. These physical principles were later combined and applied in the making of machine tools.

This entire development of technology is organically associated with and primarily responsible for the development of mankind's intellectual abilities. This is pointed out in the following explanatory paragraph from the Do-All Corporation exhibit:

> Machine tools perform in complicated ways the same basic functions and operations as hand tools. These basic functions were established by hand-held stone tools shaped by primitive man. It was through devising and using hand-wrought stone tools that mankind developed powers of mental and bodily coordination . . . and this in turn accelerated the increase in men's mental capabilities.

Such ideas about the influence of technology upon thought, taken from the publication of a respectable capitalist corporation, resemble those to be found in the writings of Marx and Engels. The thought-controllers may try to drive historical materialism out of the socialist door, but here it sneaks back in through a capitalist window.

* * *

The Do-All exhibit demonstrates that the evolution of tools can be arranged in a chronological series and ascending order, from wood and stone hand tools through metal hand tools to power-driven machine tools. Is it likewise possible to mark off corresponding successive stages in social organization?

Historical materialism answers this question affirmatively. On the broadest basis—and every big division of history can be broken down for special purposes into lesser ones—three main stages can be distinguished in man's rise from animality to the atomic age: savagery, barbarism, and civilization.

Napoleon said that an army marches on its stomach. This has been true of the forward march of the army of humanity. The acquisition of food has been the overriding aim of social production at all times, for men cannot survive, let alone progress, without regularly satisfying their hunger.

The principal epochs in the advancement of humanity can therefore be divided according to the decisive improvements effected in securing food supplies. Savagery, the infancy of humanity, constitutes that period when people depend for food upon what nature provides ready-made. Their food may come from plants, such as fruit or roots, from insects, birds or animals, or from seashore or sea life. At this stage, men forage for their food much like beasts of prey or grub for it like other animals—with these all-important differences: they cooperate with one another, and they employ crude tools along with other means and powers of production to assist them in "appropriating" the means of subsistence for their collective use.

The chief economic activities at this stage are foraging for food, hunting, and fishing; and they were developed in that sequence. The club and spear enable the savage to capture the raw materials for his meals, clothing, and shelter—all of which are embodied in animals on the hoof. The net catches fish and the fire prepares it for consumption. The Indians of southern California were at this stage when the first white settlers arrived two centuries ago.

Barbarism is the second stage of social organization. It was based upon the domestication of animals and the cultivation of plants. Food is now not merely *collected* but *produced.* The domestication of cattle, sheep, pigs, and other animals provided reserves of meat as well as food in the form of milk from goats and cows. The planting and growing of crops made regular and plentiful food supplies available.

In its evolution to our own century, civilized society can be divided into three main epochs: slavery, feudalism, and capitalism.

This food-producing revolution, which started in Asia from six to ten thousand years ago, relieved mankind from subjection to external nature for the first time. Up to that point humanity had had to rely upon what the natural environment contained to take care of its needs and had been dependent for survival upon completely external and uncontrollable natural conditions. Entire stocks and cultures of people arose, flourished, and then succumbed, like plant or animal species, in response to the beneficence or hostility of nature around them.

For example, about twenty to thirty thousand years ago, there arose a society centered around southern France called the Reindeer Culture. These people thrived by hunting huge reindeer and other herds that browsed upon the lush vegetation there. The drawings they made, which have been discovered in caves over the past seventy-five years, testify to the keenness of their eyes and minds and the trained sensitivity of their hands and place them among the most superb artists that have ever appeared on earth. However, when changed climatic and botanic conditions caused the reindeer herds to vanish, their entire culture, and very likely the people as well, died out.

The early hunters had no assured control over their mobile sources of food. The insecurity of savage life was largely overcome, or at least considerably reduced, with the advent of stock breeding, and especially with the development of agricultural techniques. For the first time, methods were instituted for obtaining extensive and expanding supplies of food products and fibers by systematic and sustained activities of working groups. These branches of economic activity made much larger and more compact populations possible.

These activities and their increased output provided the elements for the higher culture of barbarism. Farming and stock raising led to the development of such handicrafts as smelting and pottery, as accumulated food supplies generated the need to store and transport articles for the first time. Men became more stationary; denser populations aggregated; permanent dwellings were built; and village life sprang into existence.

In their further and final development, the economic activities under barbarism created the prerequisites for the coming of civilization. The material foundation for civilization was the capacity acquired by the most advanced peoples for the regular production of far more food and goods than were required for the physical maintenance of their members. These surpluses had two results. They permitted specific sections of the communities to engage in diversified activities other than the direct acquisition and production of the basic means of life. Such specialists as priests, nobles, kings, officials, smiths, potters, traders, builders, and other craftsmen made their appearance.

With the growth of specialization and the extension of trade, the top layers of these groups moved into strategic positions that enabled the more fortunate and powerful to appropriate large personal shares of the surplus of wealth. The drive to increase personal wealth flowing from the growing social division of labor and exchange of goods, led in time to the development of private property, the family, slavery, class divisions, commodity production on a large scale, trade, money, the city, and the territorial state with its army, police, courts, and other relations and institutions characteristic of civilization.

❋　❋　❋

In its evolution to our own century, civilized society can be divided into three main epochs: slavery, feudalism, and capitalism. Each of these is marked off by the special way in which the ruling propertied class at the head of the social setup manages to extract the surplus wealth upon which it lives from the laboring mass who directly create it. This entire period covers little more than the past five to six thousand years.

Civilization was ushered in and raised upon direct slavery. The very economic factors that broke up barbarism and made civilized life possible likewise provided the material preconditions for the use of slave labor. The division of labor based upon tending herds, raising crops, mining metals, and fashioning goods for sale enabled the most advanced societies to produce more than the actual laborers required for their maintenance. This made slavery both possible and profitable for the first time. It gave the most powerful stimulus to the predatory appetites of individual possessors of the means of production who strove to acquire and increase their surpluses of wealth. Slave production and ownership became the economic foundation of a new type of social organization, the source of supreme power, prestige, and privileges. And it eventually reshaped the whole structure of civilized life.

Chattel slavery was an extremely significant human contrivance—and it is distinctively human. Animals may feed upon carcasses of other animals, but they do not live upon the surpluses they create. Although we rightly recoil against any manifestations of servitude today and burn to abolish its last vestiges, it should be recognized that in its heyday slavery had imperative reasons for existence and persistence.

Science demands that every phenomenon be approached, analyzed, and appraised with objectivity, setting aside personal reactions of admiration or abhorrence. Historical materialism has to explain why slavery came to be adopted by the most advanced contingents of mankind. The principal reason was that, along with the private ownership of the means of production and the widening exchange of its products, slave labor increased the forces of production, multiplied wealth, comforts and culture—although only for the lucky few—and, on the whole, spurred mankind forward for an entire historical period. Without the extension of slave labor, there would not have been incentives unremitting enough to pile up wealth on a sizable scale that could then be applied to further the productive processes.

The historical necessity for slavery can be illustrated along two lines. The peoples who failed to adopt slave labor likewise did not proceed to civilization, however excellent their other qualities and deeds. They remained below that level because their economy lacked the inner drive of the force of greed and the dynamic propulsion arising from the slaveholder's need to exploit the slave to augment his wealth. That is a negative demonstration.

But there is more positive proof. Those states based on some form of servitude, such as the most brilliant cultures of antiquity from Babylon and Egypt to Greece and Rome, also contributed the most to the civilizing processes, from wheeled carts and the plow to writing and philosophy. These societies stood in the main line of social progress.

But if slavery had sufficient reasons for becoming the beginning and basis of ancient civilization, in turn and in time it generated the conditions and forces which would undermine and overthrow it. Once slavery became the predominant form of production either in industry, as in Greece, or in agriculture, as in Rome, it no longer furthered the development of agricultural techniques, craftsmanship, trade, or navigation. The slave empires of antiquity stagnated and disintegrated until after a lapse of centuries they were replaced by two main types of feudal organization: Asiatic and West European.

As the result of a long list of technological and other social advances, merging with a sequence of exceptional historical circumstances, feudalized Europe became the nursery for the next great stage of class society, capitalism. How and why did capitalism originate?

Once money had arisen from the extension of trading several thousand years ago, its use as capital became possible. Merchants could add to their wealth by buying goods cheap and selling them dear; moneylenders and mortgage holders could gain interest on sums advanced on the security of land or other collateral. These practices were common in both slave and feudal societies.

But if money could be used in precapitalist times to return more than the original investment, other conditions had to be fulfilled before capitalism could become established as a separate and definite world economic system. The central condition was a special kind of transaction regularly repeated on a growing scale. Large numbers of propertyless workers had to hire themselves to the possessors of money and the other means of production in order to earn a livelihood.

Hiring and firing seem to us a normal way of carrying on production. But such peoples as the Indians never knew it. Before the Europeans came, no Indian ever worked for a boss (the word itself was imported by the Dutch), because they possessed their own means of livelihood. The slave may have been purchased, but he belonged to and worked for the master his whole life long. The feudal serf or tenant was likewise bound for life to the lord and his land.

The epoch-making innovation upon which capitalism rested was the institution of working for wages as the dominant relation of production. Most of you have gone into the labor market, to an employment agency or personnel office, to get a buyer for your labor power. The employer buys this power at prevailing wage rates by the hour, day, or week and then applies it under his supervision to produce commodities that his company subsequently sells at a profit. That profit is derived from the fact that wage workers produce more value than the capitalist pays for their labor.

Up to the twentieth century, this mechanism for pumping surplus labor out of the working masses and transferring the surpluses of wealth they create to the personal credit of the capitalist was the mightiest accelerator of the productive forces and the expansion of civilization. As a distinct economic system, capitalism is only about 450 years old; it has conquered the world and journeyed from dawn to twilight in that time. This is a short life-span compared to savagery, which stretched over a million years or more, or to barbarism, which prevailed for four thousand to five thousand years. Obviously, the processes of social transformation have been considerably speeded up in modern times.

Capitalism has produced many things, good and bad, in the course of its evolution. But the most vital and valuable of all the social forces it has created is the industrial working class.

This speeding up in social progress is due in large measure to the very nature of capitalism, which continually revolutionizes its techniques of production and the entire range of social relations issuing from them. Since its birth, world capitalism has passed through three such phases of internal transformation. In its formative period, the merchants were the dominant class of capitalists because trade was the main source of wealth accumulation. Under commercial capitalism, industry and agriculture, the pillars of production, were not usually carried on by wage labor but by means of small handicrafts, peasant farming, slave or serf labor.

The industrial age was launched around the beginning of the nineteenth century with the application of steam power to the first mechanized processes, concentrating large numbers of wage workers into factories. The capitalist captains of this large-scale industry became masters of the field of production and later of entire countries and continents as their riches, their legions of wage laborers, social and political power, swelled to majestic proportions.

This vigorous, expanding, progressive, confident, competitive stage of industrial capitalism dominated the nineteenth century. It passed over into the monopoly-ridden capitalism of the twentieth century, which has carried all the basic tendencies of capitalism, and especially its most reactionary features, to extremes in economic, political, cultural, and international relations. While the processes of production have become more centralized, more rationalized, more socialized, the means of production and the wealth of the world have become concentrated in giant financial and industrial combines. So far as the capitalist sectors of society are involved, this process has been brought to the point where the capitalist monopolies of a single country, the U.S., dictate to all the rest.

✳   ✳   ✳

The most important question to be asked at this point is: What is the destiny of the development of civilization in its capitalist form? Disregarding in-between views, which at bottom evade the answer, two irreconcilable viewpoints assert themselves, corresponding to the world outlooks of two opposing classes. The spokesmen for capitalism say that nothing more remains to be done except to perfect their system as it stands, and it can roll on and on and on. The Do-All Corporation, for example, which published so instructive a chart on the evolution of tools, declares that more and better machine tools, which they hope will be bought at substantial profit from their company, will guarantee continued progress and prosperity for capitalist America without the least change in existing class relations.

Socialists give a completely different answer based upon an incomparably more penetrating, correct, and comprehensive analysis of the movement of history, the structure of capitalism, and the struggles presently agitating the world around us. The historical function of capitalism is not to perpetuate itself indefinitely but to create the conditions and prepare the forces that will bring about its own replacement by a more efficient form of material production and a higher type of social organization. Just as capitalism supplanted feudalism and slavery, and civilization swept aside savagery and barbarism, so the time has come for capitalism itself to be superseded. How and by whom is this revolutionary transformation to be effected?

In the last century, Marx made a scientific analysis of the workings of the capitalist system which explained how its inner contradictions would bring about its downfall. The revolutions of our own century since 1917 are demonstrating in real life that capitalism is due to be relegated to the museum of antiquities. It is worthwhile to understand the inexorable underlying causes of these developments, which appear so inexplicable and abhorrent to the upholders of the capitalist system.

Capitalism has produced many things, good and bad, in the course of its evolution. But the most vital and valuable of all the social forces it has created is the industrial working class. The capitalist class has brought into existence a vast army of wage laborers, centralized and disciplined, and set it into motion for its own purposes, to make and operate the machines, factories, and all the other production and transportation facilities from which its profits emanate.

The exploitation and abuses, inherent and inescapable in the capitalist organization of economic life, provoke the workers time and again to organize themselves and undertake militant action to defend their elementary interests. The struggle between these conflicting social classes is today the dominant and driving force of world and American history, just as the conflict between the bourgeois-led forces against the precapitalist elements was the motivating force of history in the immediately preceding centuries.

The current struggle, which has been gathering momentum and expanding its scope for a hundred years, has entered its decisive phase on a world scale. Except for Cuba, the preliminary battles between the procapitalist and the anticapitalist forces have so far been waged to a conclusion in countries outside the Western Hemisphere. Sooner or later, however, they are bound to break out and be fought to a finish within this country, which is not only the stronghold of capitalist power but also the home of the best-organized and technically most proficient working class on this globe.

The main line of development in America, no less than the course of world history, points to such a conclusion. Why is this so?

2

The main course of American history and its next stage

We have reviewed the course by which humanity climbed out of the animal state, and we have marked the successive steps in that climb. Mankind had to crawl through savagery for a million years or more, walk through barbarism, and then, with shoulders hunched and head bowed, enter the iron gates of class society. There, for thousands of years, mankind endured a harsh schooling under the rod and rule of private property, which began with slavery and reached its highest form in capitalist civilization. Now our own age stands, or rather struggles, at the entrance to socialism.

Let us now pass from the historical progress of mankind, viewed as a whole, to inspect one of its parts, the United States of North America. Because U.S. imperialism is the mainstay of the international capitalist system, the role of the American people is crucial in deciding how quickly and how well humanity crosses the great divide between the class society of the past and the reorganization and reinvigoration of the world along socialist lines.

I shall try to give brief answers to the following four questions: What has been the course of American history in its essentials? What are its connections with the march of the rest of humankind? What has been the outcome to date? Finally, where do we fit into the picture?

❋ ❋ ❋

American history breaks sharply into two fundamentally different epochs. One belongs to the aboriginal inhabitants, the Indians; the other starts with the coming of white Europeans to America at the end of the fifteenth century. The beginnings of human activity in the Western Hemisphere are still obscure. But it is surmised that from twenty to thirty thousand years ago, early Stone Age Asiatics, thanks to favorable climatic conditions which united that part of Alaska with Siberia, crossed over the Bering Strait and slowly made their way throughout North, Central, and South America. Later streams of migration may have brought the practices of gardening with them. It is upon these bequests that the Indians fashioned their type of existence.

Whoever regards the Indians as insignificant or incompetent has defective historical judgment. Humanity has been raised to its present estate by four branches of productive activity. The first is food gathering, which includes grubbing for roots and berries as well as hunting and fishing. The second is stock raising. The third is agriculture. The fourth is craftsmanship, graduating into large-scale industry.

The Indians were extremely adept at hunting, fishing, and other ways of food gathering. They were ingenious craftsmen whose work in some fields has never been excelled. The Incas, for example, made textiles which were extremely fine in texture, coloring, and design. They invented and used more different techniques of weaving on their hand looms than any other people in history.

However, the Indians showed the greatest talent in their development of agriculture. They may even have independently invented soil cultivation. In any case they brought it to diversified perfection. We are indebted to the Indians for most of the vegetables that today come from the fields and through the kitchens onto our tables. Most important are corn, potatoes, and beans, but there is in addition a considerable list including tomatoes, chili, pineapples, peanuts, avocados, and for after-dinner purposes, tobacco. They knew and used the properties of four hundred separate species of plants. No plant cultivated by the American Indians was known to Asia, Europe, or Africa prior to the white invasion of America.

Much is heard about all that white men brought over to the Indians, but little about what the Indians gave the European whites. The introduction of the food plants taken from the Indians more than doubled the available food supply of the older continent after the fifteenth century and became an important factor in the expansion of capitalist civilization. Over half of the agricultural produce raised in the world today comes from plants domesticated by the Indians!

From the first to the fifteenth centuries, the Indians themselves created magnificent, even astounding cultures on the basis of their achievements in agriculture. Agriculture enabled some of the scattered and roving hunting tribes of Indians to aggregate in small but permanent settlements where they supported themselves by growing corn, beans, and other vegetables. They also raised and wove cotton, made pottery, and developed other handicrafts.

The Incas of the Andes, the Mayans of Guatemala and Yucatán, and the Aztecs of central Mexico, unaffected by European civilization and having developed independently, constituted the most advanced of the Indian societies. Their cultures embodied the utmost the Indians were able to accomplish within the twenty-five thousand years or so allotted them by history. In fact, the Mayans had made mathematical and astronomical calculations more complex and advanced than those of the European invaders. They had independently invented the zero for use in their number system—something even the Greeks and Romans had lacked.

Whoever regards the Indians as insignificant or incompetent has defective historical judgment.

Indians progressed as far as the middle stage of barbarism and were stopped there. Whether or not, given unlimited time and no interference from more powerful and productive peoples, they would have mounted all the way to civilization must remain unanswered. This much can be stated: they had formidable obstacles to overcome along such a path. The Indians did not have such important domesticated animals as the horse, cow, pig, sheep, or water buffalo that had pulled the Asians and Europeans along toward civilization. They had only the dog, turkey, guinea pig, and, in the Andean highlands, llamas, alpacas, and, in some places, bees. Moreover, they did not use the wheel, except for toys, did not know the use of iron or firearms, and did not have other prerequisites for civilizing themselves.

However, history in the other part of the globe settled this question without further appeal. For, while the most advanced Indians had been moving up from wandering hunters' lives to those of settlers in barbaric communities, the Europeans, themselves an offspring of Asiatic culture, had not only entered class society but had become highly civilized. Their most progressive segments along the Atlantic seaboard were passing over from feudalism to capitalism.

This uneven development of society in the Old World and the New provided the historical setting for the second great turning point in American history. What was the essential meaning of the upheaval initiated by the west European crossing of the Atlantic? It represented the transition from the Stone Age to the Iron Age in America, from barbaric to civilized modes of life, from tribal organization based upon collectivist practices to a society rooted in private property, production for exchange, the family, the state, and so forth.

Few spectacles in history are more dramatic and instructive than the confrontation and conflict between the Indian representatives of communal Stone Age life and the armed agents of class civilization. Science fiction tells about visitations to this planet by Martians in flying saucers. To the Indians, the first visitations of the white men were no less startling and incomprehensible.

To the Indians, these white men had completely alien customs, standards, and ways of life. They were strange in appearance and behavior. In fact, the differences between the two were so profound as to be irreconcilable. What was the root cause of the enduring and deadly clash between them? They represented two utterly incompatible levels of social organization that had grown out of and were based upon dissimilar conditions and were heading toward entirely different goals.

Even at its height, Indian life was based upon tribal collectivism and its crude technology. Indian psychology was fashioned by such social institutions. The Indians not only did not have the wheel, iron, or the alphabet—they also lacked the institutions, ideas, feelings, and aims of civilized peoples who had been molded by the technology and culture of an acquisitive society. These conditions had stamped out a very special kind of human being as the peculiar product of civilization based upon private ownership.

The most highly developed Indians subsisted on agriculture. But their agriculture was not of the same economic mode as that of the newcomers. The major means of producing food by soil cultivation belonged to the entire tribe and nothing in its production or distribution could be exclusively claimed by individual owners. This was true of the principal means of production, the land itself. When the Europeans arrived at these shores, all the way from the Atlantic to the Pacific there was not a single foot of ground that a person could stand on and assert: "This belongs to my solitary private self, or to my little family—all others keep off and stay out." The land belonged to the whole people.

It was quite otherwise with the white men, the bearers of the new and higher type of society. To them it appeared natural and necessary, as it still does to most citizens of this country, that almost everything on earth should pass into someone's private ownership. Clothes, houses, weapons of war, tools, ships, even human beings themselves, could be bought and sold.

It was in the shiny embodiment of precious metals that private property became not only the cornerstone of worldly existence but even opened up the gates of heaven. Columbus wrote to Queen Isabella as follows: "Gold constitutes treasure and he who possesses it has all he needs in this world as also the means of rescuing souls from purgatory and restoring them to the enjoyment of paradise." This was literally true at that time because rich Catholics could buy indulgences for their sins from the Pope. Cortez is said to have told some natives of Mexico: "We Spaniards are troubled with a disease of the heart for which we find gold, and gold only, a specific remedy."

The doctrine of the European whites was that everything must have its price, whether it pertains to present happiness or future salvation. This idea remains the guideline for the plutocratic rulers of our own day, who in their campaigns to dominate the world not only buy up individuals but even whole governments. In their quest for gold and lust for gain, Columbus and the conquistadores enslaved and killed thousands of West Indians in the islands they discovered. And that was only the beginning.

Viewed from the heights of world history, this turning point in America was characterized by the conjuncture of two revolutionary processes. The first was the shift of maritime Europe from a feudal to a bourgeois basis. Part of this revolutionizing of

Western Europe was a push outward as the capitalist traders extended their operations throughout the globe. Their exploring, marketing, pirating expeditions brought the emissaries of the budding bourgeois society in Europe across the ocean and into collision with the Indians. The rape of the ancient cultures of the Aztecs and Incas, the enslavement and extermination of the natives by the Spanish conquerors and others, was a collateral offensive of this European revolution on our own continent.

Science fiction tells about visitations to this planet by Martians in flying saucers. To the Indians, the first visitations of the white men were no less startling and incomprehensible.

Through the extension of the revolutionary process, the peoples of the Stone Age here were overcome and supplanted by the most advanced representatives of class civilization. This was not the only continent on which such a process took place. What happened from the fifteenth to the nineteenth centuries in the New World had taken place much earlier in western Europe itself; and it was to reach into the most remote sectors of the world, as capitalism has spread over the earth from that time to our own.

The contest between the Stone Age peoples and the representatives of the bourgeois epoch was fiercely fought. Their wars stretched over four centuries and ended in the disintegration, dispossession, or destruction of the prehistoric cultures and the unchallenged supremacy of class society.

With the advent of the white Europeans (as well as the enslaved colored Africans who were transported here by them), American history was switched onto an entirely different set of rails, a new course marked out by the needs of a young, expanding world capitalism.

We come now to a most crucial question: What has been the main line of American growth since 1492? Various answers are given—the growth of national independence, the spread of democracy, the coming into his own of the common man, or the expansion of industry. Each of these familiar formulas taught in the schools does record some aspect of the process, but none goes to the heart of the matter.

The correct answer to the question is that despite detours en route, the main line of American history has consisted in the construction and consolidation of capitalist civilization, which has been carried to its ultimate in our own day. Any attempt to explain the development of American society since the sixteenth century will be brought up against this fact. The discovery, exploration, settlement, cultivation, exploitation, democratization, and industrialization of this continent must all be seen as successive steps in promoting the building of bourgeois society. This is the only interpretation of the decisive events in the past 450 years in North America that makes sense, gives continuity and coherence to our complex history, distinguishes the mainstream from tributaries, and is validated by the development of American society. Everything in our national history has to be referred to, and linked up with, the process of establishing the capitalist way of life in its most pronounced and, today, its most pernicious form.

This is commonly called "The American Way of Life." A more realistic and honest characterization would be the capitalist way of life because, as I shall indicate, this is destined to be only a historically limited and passing expression of civilized life in America.

The central importance of the formation and transformation of bourgeois society can be demonstrated in another way. What is the most outstanding peculiarity of American history since the coming of the Europeans? There have been many peculiarities in the history of this country; in some ways this is a very peculiar country. But what marks off American life from the development of the other great nations of the world is that the growth and construction of American society falls entirely within the epoch of the expansion of capitalism on a global scale. That is the key to understanding American history, whether you deal with colonial history, nineteenth-century history, or twentieth-century history.

When the Europeans arrived at these shores, all the way from the Atlantic to the Pacific there was not a single foot of ground that a person could stand on and assert: 'This belongs to my solitary private self. . . .' The land belonged to the whole people.

It is not true of other leading countries such as England, Germany, Russia, India, Japan, or China. These countries passed through prolonged periods of slave or feudal civilization that left their stamp upon them to this very day. Look at MacArthur's preservation of that feudal relic, the emperor of Japan, or that Sunday supplement delight, the monarchy of England.

America, on the other hand, leaped from savagery and barbarism to capitalism, tipping its hat along the way to slavery and feudalism, which held no more than subordinate places in building the bourgeois system. In a couple of centuries, the American people hurried through stages of social development that took the rest of mankind many thousands of years. But there was close interconnection between these two processes. If the rest of mankind had not already made these acquisitions, we Americans would not have been able to rush ahead so far and so fast. The tasks of pioneers are invariably harder and take far longer to accomplish.

The fusion of the antifeudal revolution in Europe with the wars of extermination against the Indians ushered in the bourgeois epoch of American history. This period has stretched over

450 years. It falls into three distinct phases, each marked off by revolutionary changes in American life.

* * *

The first period is that of colonial America, which extended from 1500 to the passage of the U.S. Constitution in 1788–89. If we analyze the social forms and economic forces of American life during these three centuries, colonial America, the formative period of our civilization, stands out as an exceptional blending of precapitalist agencies with the oncoming capitalist forms and forces of production. The tribal collectivism of the Indians was being transformed, pushed back, annihilated; remnants of feudalism were imported from Europe and transplanted here. The ranchos of southern California in the early nineteenth century had been preceded by colonial baronies; entire colonies such as Maryland and Pennsylvania were owned by landed proprietors who had been given title to them by the English monarchy. Big planters exploited white indentured servants and colored chattel slaves who in many places provided the main labor forces.

Alongside them were hundreds of thousands of small farmers, hunters, trappers, artisans, traders, merchants, and others associated with the new forms of ownership and economic activity and animated by customs, feelings, and ideas stemming from the capitalism which was advancing in Europe and now beginning to flourish on this side of the Atlantic.

The fundamental question posed by this development was—which would prevail, the precapitalist or the capitalist forces? This was the axis of the social struggles within the colonies and even of the incessant wars for possession of the New World among the European nations, which characterized the colonial period. The showdown on this front came in the years between 1763 and 1789, the period of the preparation, outbreak, waging, and conclusion of the first American revolution. This was the first stage of the bourgeois-democratic revolution on this continent.

It assumed the form of a war between the rulers and supporters of Great Britain and the colonial masses led by representatives of the Northern merchants, bankers, manufacturers, and planters of the Southern slave system, which was an appendage of growing native capitalism. The outcome of the contest determined the next stage in the destiny of American capitalism. If Great Britain's domination had persisted, that may have stunted and perverted the further development of bourgeois society here as it did in India and Africa.

The first American revolution and its war for independence was a genuine people's movement. Such movements destroy much that has become rotten and is ready for burial. But, above all, they are socially creative, bringing to birth institutions that provide the ways and means for the next surge forward. That was certainly true of our first national revolution, which is permanently embedded in the American and international consciousness. So powerful and persistent are its traditions that they are today a source of embarrassment to the capitalist rulers of this country in their dealings with the colonial movements for emancipation.

What were the notable achievements of this first stage of the North American bourgeois-democratic revolution? It overthrew the reactionary rule of the ten thousand merchants, bankers, landowners, and manufacturers of Great Britain, who, after helping to spur the American colonies forward, had become the biggest block to their further advance. It gave independence to the colonies, unified them, and cleared away such feudal vestiges as the crown lands which the monarchy held. It democratized the states and gave them a republican form of government. It cleared the ground for a swift expansion of civilization in its native capitalist forms from the Atlantic to the Pacific.

The revolution had international repercussions. It inspired and protected similar movements during the next century in the Latin American colonies and even radiated back to the Old Continent. Read the diary of Gouverneur Morris, a financial leader of the Patriot Party, who became one of the early U.S. ambassadors to France. He was in Paris selling American properties to aristocrats who were threatened with exile by the French revolution. These clients complained to the sympathetic Morris that if only his countrymen had refrained from revolution, the French people would never have had the notion or courage to follow suit.

But even the most thoroughgoing revolution cannot do more than historical possibilities permit. Two serious shortcomings in the work of this first upheaval manifested themselves in the next decades. One was the fact that the revolution did not and could not eliminate the soil in which the institution of slavery was rooted. Many leaders of the time, among them Thomas Jefferson, hoped that slavery would wither away because of unfavorable economic conditions.

The second shortcoming was that although the revolt gave Americans political independence, it could not give thoroughgoing independence to the U.S. in a capitalist sense. This was true in two ways: at home the Northern capitalists had to share power with the Southern slaveowners, with whom they had waged the revolutionary war for independence and set up the new government; on the international market they remained in economic subordination to the more advanced industrial and financial structure of England.

The leaders of the revolution were aware of these deficiencies. The same Gouverneur Morris wrote to President George Washington from Paris on September 30, 1791:

> We shall . . . make great and rapid progress in useful manufactures. This alone is wanting to compleat our independence. We shall then be as it were a World by ourselves, and far from the Jars and Wars of Europe, their various revolutions will serve merely to instruct and amuse. Like the roaring of a Tempestuous Sea, which at a certain distance becomes a pleasing Sound.

However, a historical freak came along, which upset this pleasant prospect. This freak was the result of a double revolution in technology, one which took place in Europe, especially in English industry, and the other in American agriculture. The establishment of factories with steam-driven machinery in English industry, notably in textiles, its most important branch, created the demand for large supplies of cotton. The invention of the cotton gin enabled the Southern planters to supply that demand.

Consequently, slavery, which had been withering on the vine, acquired a new lease on life. This economic combination invested the nobles of the Southern cotton kingdom with tremendous wealth and power. A study of American history in the first half of the nineteenth century shows that its national and political life was dominated and directed by the struggle for supremacy waged by the forces centered around the Southern slaveholders on one side and those of the antislavery elements on the other. The crucial social issue before the nation was not always stated bluntly. But when every other conflict was traced to its roots, it was found to be connected with the question: What are we Americans going to do about slavery?

(A similar situation exists today in relation to capitalism. No matter what dispute agitates the political-economic life of this country, it sooner or later brings up the great social-economic question: What are we Americans going to do about capitalism?)

For the first fifty years of the nineteenth century, the cotton aristocrats of the South undeniably held center stage. They became very cocky about their power and privileges, which they thought would last indefinitely. Then, around 1850, conditions began to change quite rapidly. A new combination of social forces appeared that was to prove strong enough not only to challenge the slave power but to meet it in civil war, conquer and eliminate it.

It is highly instructive to study the mentality and outlook of the American people in 1848. That was a year of revolutions in the principal countries of western Europe. The people in the

United States, including its governing groups, viewed these outbursts in an isolationist spirit.

The European revolutions even pleased certain sections of the ruling classes in the United States because they were directed mainly against monarchies. There were no monarchies here to overthrow, although there was a slave aristocracy rooted in the South. Although most of the common people in the United States sympathized with the European revolutions, they looked upon them as no more than a catching up with what had already been achieved in this country. The Americans said to themselves: "We've already had our revolution and don't need any more here. The quota of revolutions assigned to us by history is exhausted."

Every schoolchild knows that the slave power was abolished. But the principal achievement of this revolution from the standpoint of American and world development was that the last of the internal impediments to the march of American capitalism were leveled, and the way cleared for the consolidation of capitalist rule.

They did not see even fifteen years into their own future. The bourgeois-democratic revolution still had considerable unfinished business. During the 1850s, it became plainer that the Southern slaveholders were not only tightening their autocracy in the Southern states but were trying to make slaves of the entire population of the United States. This small set of rich men arrogated to themselves the right to tell the people what they could and could not do, where the country should expand, and how the affairs of America should and should not be managed.

So a second revolution proved necessary to complete those tasks left unsettled in the late eighteenth century and to dispose of the main problems that had confronted the American people in the meantime. There had to be thirteen years of preparatory struggles, four and a half years of civil war, twelve years of Reconstruction—about thirty years in all, in this intense and inescapable revolutionary upheaval.

What is most important for us now are the net results of that travail. Every schoolchild knows that the slave power was abolished and the Negro population unshackled from chattel slavery. But the principal achievement of this revolution from the standpoint of American and world development was that the last of the internal impediments to the march of American capitalism were leveled, and the way cleared for the consolidation of capitalist rule.

That period saw the conclusion of the contest that had been going on since 1492 between the procapitalist and precapitalist forces on this continent. See what had happened to the peoples representing the diverse precapitalist ways of life. The Indians, who embodied savagery and barbarism, had either been exterminated, dispossessed, or herded into reservations. England, which had upheld feudalism and colonial subjugation, had been swept aside and American industrial capital had attained not only political supremacy but economic independence. The Southern plantation owners, who were the final formidable precapitalist force to be pushed out of the road, had been smashed and expropriated by the Civil War and Reconstruction.

The capitalist rulers of the industrial system were then like the Count of Monte Cristo when he burst from prison and exclaimed, with so much wealth and newly gained liberty at his command, "The world is mine!" And they have been acting on that premise ever since.

* * *

I would like now to make several observations on the economic and political development of American society from 1492 to the triumph of the capitalist class. As has already been pointed out, private property in the means of production was virtually nonexistent on this continent until the fifteenth century. Thereafter, as the white settlers spread, the dominant trend was for all the means of production to pass into private hands and be exploited along such lines. The land, for example, which had been tribally held, was cut up and appropriated by individuals or corporations from one end of the country to the other.

After the victory of the Northern bankers, merchants, and manufacturers in the middle of the nineteenth century, this process moved on to a still higher plane. The means of production under private ownership became more and more concentrated in corporate hands. Today an individual might be able to build a single auto or airplane, but without many, many millions of dollars he would not be able to compete in the market with General Motors or Ford or Lockheed or Douglas. Even so big a magnate as Henry J. Kaiser found that out in auto.

Today there is hardly an acre of land without its title deed. In fact, the Civil War promoted this process through the Homestead Act, which gave 160 acres to private individuals, and through other acts of Congress that handed over millions of acres to railroad corporations. Insofar as the land was distributed to small farmers, this was progressive because it was the only way to hasten the development of agriculture under the given conditions.

It is impossible to detail here the settlement and building of the Midwest and the West, but certain consequences of capitalist expansion deserve mention. First, as a result of this capitalist expansion, the minds of average Americans, unlike those of the Indians, have been so molded by the institutions of private property that its standards can be thrown off only with difficulty. The Europeans penetrated the America of the Indians; and their descendants are venturing into outer space. One extreme, absurd, but for that very reason most instructive, illustration of the effects of capitalist expansion on American consciousness appeared in a press dispatch from Illinois with the headline: "Who Is the

Owner of Outer-Space; Chicagoan Insists that He Is." This news item followed:

> With plans for launching man-made earth satellites now in motion, the question was inevitable [inevitable, that is, to Americans believing in the sacredness of private ownership]: Who owns outer space?
>
> Most experts agreed that the question was over their heads. The rocket scientists said it was a problem for the international law experts. The lawyers said they had no precedents to go by. Only James T. Mangan, a fast-thinking Chicago press agent, has a firm answer to the question of space sovereignty. Mangan declares he owns outer space. To back up his claim, he has a deed filed with the Cook County (Chicago) Recorder. The deed, accepted after the state's attorney's office solemnly upheld the claim in a four-page legal opinion, seized "all space in all directions from the earth at midnight," December 20, 1948.
>
> Mangan declared that the statute of limitations for challenging the deed expires December 20, 1955, and added: "The government has no legal right to space without my permission."

If this be madness, yet there is method in it. That method is the mainspring of the capitalist way of life. This gentleman, Mangan, is only logically extending to the exploration of outer space the same acquisitive creed which guided our founding fathers in taking over the American continent. This particular fanatic of private property thinks the same law is going to apply no matter how far into space we fly and no matter how far we go into the future. He differs from other exponents of capitalism only in the boldness and consistency of his private-property logic.

The second point I want to deal with is the interconnection between evolution and revolution. These two phases of social development are often opposed to each other as unconnected opposites, irreconcilable alternatives. What does American history teach us about them? The American people have already passed through two revolutionary periods in their national history, each the culmination of lengthy periods of social progress on the basis of previous achievements.

During the interval between revolutions, relatively small changes gradually occurred in people's lives. They consequently took the given framework of their lives for granted, viewed it as fixed and final, and found it hard to imagine a different way. The idea of revolutionary change in their own lives and lifetimes seemed fantastic or at least irrelevant. Yet it was during those very periods of evolutionary progress that often unnoticed accumulations of changes prepared more drastic change.

The new class interests, which grew powerful but remained unsatisfied, the social and political conflicts, which recurred but remained unresolved, the shifts in the relations of antagonistic social forces kept asserting themselves in a series of disturbances until they reached an acute stage. The people of this country were not reckless. They made every attempt to find reasonable compromises between the contending forces, and often arrived at them. But after a while, these truces turned out to be ineffectual and short-lived. The irrepressible conflict of social forces broke out at higher stages until the breaking point was reached.

Look at the American colonists of 1763. They had just emerged—side-by-side with mother England—from a successful war against the French and the Indians. They did not anticipate that within ten years they would be fighting for their own freedom against England and alongside the very French monarchy they had fought in 1763. That would have been considered fantastic. Yet it happened only a little more than a decade later. Dr. Benjamin Rush, one of Pennsylvania's signers of the Declaration of Independence, observed in his *Autobiography* that:

> Not one man in a thousand contemplated or wished for the independence of our country in 1774, and but few of

those who assented to it, foresaw the immense influence it would soon have upon the national and individual characters of the Americans.

So, too, the majority of Northerners, who enjoyed the economic boom in America from 1851 to 1857—the biggest boom in the nineteenth century preceding the Civil War—little reckoned that as the result of domestic processes accelerated by that very prosperity, the country was going to be split on the slave question four years after the depression of 1857. Instead, they reasoned: Hadn't there been a compromise with the slaveholders in 1850—and couldn't others be arrived at? Indeed, there were attempts at compromise up to the very outbreak of the Civil War, and even afterwards.

Of course, the Abolitionists at one extreme and the Southern "Fire-Eaters" at the other prophesied a different course of development and, in their own ways, prepared for the coming revolution. But these radical voices on the left and the right were few and far between.

The first American revolution occurred during the era of commercial capitalism, which was the first stage in world capitalist development. . . . The second American revolution took place at the time of the greatest expansion of industrial capitalism on both sides of the Atlantic.

These crucial episodes in American history demonstrate that, under conditions of class society, periods of gradual social *evolution* prepare forces for the *revolutionary* solution of the accumulated and unfinished problems of peoples and nations. This revolutionary cleanup in turn creates the premises for a new and higher stage of evolutionary progress. This alternation is demonstrated with exceptional clarity by American history in the eighteenth and nineteenth centuries.

It is important to note, as a third point in dealing with the consequences of capitalist development in the United States, that our national revolutions stemmed directly from native conditions. Neither was imported by "outside agitators," although some, like Tom Paine, played important roles. They came from the ripening of conflicts between internal social forces. But this is only one side of the matter. The domestic struggles in turn were connected with, conditioned, and determined by world economic and social development.

We pointed out earlier that the impetus for the overseas migration that changed the face of America came from the antifeudal bourgeois revolutions, which were transforming Europe; the conquest of our continent was an offshoot of those revolutions. The first American revolution occurred during the era of commercial capitalism, which was the first stage in world capitalist development. Historically, it forms part of the series of bourgeois-democratic revolutions by which the capitalist class came to power on an international scale. The first American revolution must be considered a child of the English bourgeois revolution of the mid-seventeenth century and a parent of sorts to the French bourgeois-democratic revolution of the late eighteenth century.

Trade in this era, not simply American but world trade, produced a powerful merchant class in the North, which was backed up by maritime workers and artisans in the coastal cities and by free farmers in the countryside. These became the shock troops of the Sons of Liberty. It is no accident that the bustling seaport of Boston, populated by rich merchants who wanted to get out from under the thumb of Great Britain and by robust waterfront workers, longshoremen, and sailors, stood in the forefront of the fight against Great Britain and that the revolutionary war itself was detonated by the British efforts to gag and strangle Boston.

The second American revolution took place at the time of the greatest expansion of industrial capitalism on both sides of the Atlantic. The years from 1848 to 1871 were punctuated by wars and revolutions. These conflicts did not mark the disintegration of world capital, as they do in the present century, but finally gave the capitalist class unmitigated supremacy in America and a series of countries in Europe.

The second stage of the bourgeois-democratic revolution in the United States, the Civil War, placed the Northern industrialists in the saddle. It was the outstanding revolutionary event of the entire period from 1848 to 1871, which began with the abortive French and German revolutions of 1848 and ended with the Franco-Prussian War and the Paris Commune of 1871. The decisive event of that period in world history was the U.S. capitalists' victory in this country, which heralded their ascent to world power.

*　　*　　*

With these lessons in mind, let us now look at the march of American society from the close of the Civil War period until today. Having reaped the fruits of two successful revolutions, the capitalists began to enjoy them. For them, revolution in America was a thing of the past; the United States would advance by small slow steps. Indeed, there has been a significant evolution of capitalist society on the foundation of the achievements of its previous revolutions. But in the dialectic of our national development, it is the very extraordinary expansion of the capitalist forces of production that has been preparing the elements for another, and this time a final, showdown between class forces that belong to different stages of economic and social evolution.

Since 1878, there have been two major trends in operation in this country. The predominant one to date has been the growing concentration of economic, political, and cultural power in the hands of the monopolists. They have occasionally been challenged but never dislodged. Today they are open and insolent in the exercise of power. As Mr. Wilson of the biggest monopoly and the Defense Department has said: "What's good for General Motors is good for the country."

This echoes the assertion by an earlier absolute monarch, Louis XIV: "I am the state." The old regime of France had its funeral in 1789. Everything in this world—and this is especially true of political regimes and social systems under class society—includes within itself its own opposition, its own fatal opposition. This is certainly true of the power of capitalism which breeds its own nemesis in the productive—and political—capacities of wage labor.

For many years, despite occasional tiffs, the American colonists got along with their mother country and even cherished the tie. Then came a very rapid and radical reversal in relations, a duel to the end.

The irony is that the greater the wealth of the capitalists, the stronger becomes the social position of the exploited workers from whom this wealth is derived. The United States has witnessed, side-by-side with the rise of monopoly capitalism, the emergence of an ever more strongly organized, centralized, and unified labor movement. Ever since the capitalists and wage workers came into existence together, there have been differences, friction, outbursts of conflict, strikes, lockouts, between sections of these two classes. They arise from the very nature of their relations, which are antagonistic.

By and large, up to now, these conflicts have never gone beyond the bounds of the basic political and economic structure laid down by the Civil War. They have been subdued, reconciled, or smoothed over. Despite all disturbances, the monopolist rulers have entrenched themselves more firmly in their paramount positions. However, a closer scrutiny of the development discloses that the working class occupies an increasingly influential, though still subordinate, place in our national life.

The question presents itself with renewed force: Will this situation of class stalemate—with the workers in a secondary position—continue indefinitely? The capitalists naturally answer that it can and must be so. Furthermore, they do everything from teaching in school the perpetual existence of the established class structure to passing antilabor laws to insure the continuance of the status quo. The union officialdom, for their part, go along with this general proposition.

Neither the capitalist spokesmen nor the AFL-CIO officialdom will find any precedent in American history to reinforce their expectations of an indefinite maintenance of the status quo. That is one lesson from our national past that the "long view" of socialism emphasizes. For many years, despite occasional tiffs, the American colonists got along with their mother country and even cherished the tie. Then came a very rapid and radical reversal in relations, a duel to the end. The same held true of the long coexistence of the Northern free states and Southern slavery. For sixty years, the Northerners had to play second fiddle to the Southern slave autocracy until the majority of people in the country came to believe that this situation would endure indefinitely. The slaveowners, like the capitalists of today, taught that their "American way of life" was the crown of civilization. But once the new combination of progressive forces was obliged to assert itself, the maturing differences broke out in a civil war which disposed of the old order. The political collaborators of yesterday turned into irreconcilable foes on the morrow.

The upholders of the status quo in this country can find still less support from the main trends of world history in our own time. In 1848, at a time when the capitalist classes on both sides of the Atlantic were toppling monarchies and feudal aristocracies, the pioneer communists first publicly proclaimed their ideas and started the movement of scientific socialism, which has become the guide of the world working class in its struggle for emancipation. In 1917, sixty-nine years later, the first working-class state was set up in the Soviet Union. There was no other established for almost three decades.

Then came the Second World War, which extended the domain of collectivized property throughout Eastern Europe, and afterwards the victory of the Chinese revolution, which overturned capitalism in that major power in the East.

All this is tantamount to a colossal advance of world history. The essence of the new stage is that the movement for the advancement of capitalism, which had dominated world history from the sixteenth to the nineteenth centuries, has been succeeded on a world scale in the twentieth century by the anticapitalist movement of the socialist working class and its colonial allies.

Organized labor has within its own grasp enough political strength, not to speak of its economic and social capacities, to be the sovereign force in this country.

Of course it is not only the hope but the policy of the present capitalist holders of power that the achievements, ideas, and purposes of this revolutionary movement of the workers and colonial peoples can be contained in other parts of the world and crushed there. At any rate, the witch-hunters make every effort to keep its influences from these shores. Just as the British tyrants and the Southern slaveholders, each in their day, mustered all their resources to hold back the oncoming revolutionary forces in this land, so do the agents of the American plutocracy today. Will the monopolists succeed where their forerunners failed? Let us consider this question.

The high point of a revolutionary process consists in the transfer of supreme power from one class to another. What are the prevailing relationships of power in the United States? All basic decisions on foreign and domestic policy are made by the top capitalist circles to forward their aims and interests. Labor may be able to modify this or that decision or policy, but its influence does no more than curb the political power exercised by the monopolists.

However, there is a remarkable anomaly in such a relationship of forces. The now united union movement has about seventeen million members. With their families, followers, and friends, this movement can muster enough votes to give the political representatives of organized labor majority power in the cities, in the states, and in Washington. This means that the capitalists continue to exercise their sway by virtue of default, that is, a continued default of independent political action and organization by labor, or more precisely by its present leaders. They are failing to use one-thousandth of the power their movement presently and potentially possesses on behalf of the working people.

Organized labor has within its own grasp enough political strength, not to speak of its economic and social capacities, to be the sovereign force in this country. That is why any movement toward the formation of an independent party of labor based on the trade unions would have such highly revolutionizing implications upon the existing setup, regardless of the intentions or announced program of its organizers. Any such move on a massive scale would portend a shift in the power of supreme decision in the United States from capitalist to labor circles, just as the coming to Washington of the Republican Party in 1860 signified the shift of power away from the slaveholders to the Northern industrialists.

The Republican leaders of 1861 did not have revolutionary intentions. They headed a reformist party. They wanted to restrict the power of the slaveholders. But to do this involved upsetting the established balance of class forces. The slaveholders recognized the threat to their supremacy far more clearly and felt it more keenly than did the Northern Republican leaders themselves. That is why they initiated a counterrevolutionary assault in order to retrieve the power they had previously possessed.

The parallel with any national assumption of political power by the labor movement, even in a reformist way, is plain to see. Is such a shift possible? A succession of crucial shifts of power has marked the onward movement of the American people: from Britain to the colonial merchants and planters in the eighteenth century; and from the Southern slavocracy to the industrial capitalists in the nineteenth century. The thrust in the present period of our national history is toward another such colossal shift, this time from the ruling plutocracy to the rising working class and its allies among the oppressed minorities.

The whole course of economic, social, and political development in this country and in this century points to such a shift in power. Of course, the working class is far from predominant yet, and even less conscious of its historical mission. But, from the standpoint of the long view, it is most important to note the different rates of growth in the economic, social, and political potentialities of the respective contenders for supreme power. Reviewing this country's history from 1876 to 1957, together with the rate of growth of the working-class movement on a world scale, the balance of forces has been steadily shifting, despite all oscillations, toward the side of working-class power. Nothing whatsoever, including imperialist war, the Taft-Hartley Act, and McCarthyism, has been able to stop the momentum of the U.S. labor movement.

The supreme merit of scientific socialism is that it enables us to participate in this process by understanding it, by striving to influence it through all its stages, by giving it proper direction and speeding it up so that its great aims can be achieved most economically and efficiently. This job can be done in an organized fashion only through a revolutionary leadership and a Marxist party that understands its indispensable educational and organizational functions in the process.

* * *

Let us now return to Vincent Sheean, who popularized the phrase "the long view of history" and was the point of departure for these remarks. Sad to say, this writer held the long view for a very short time. Uplifted by the revolutionary events of the 1920s, and transformed by the widespread radicalism of the 1930s, he had become a well-wisher of the socialist transformation of society, in his own way a partisan of the anti-imperialist cause, and even a sympathizer of Leninism. But, as the backward sweep in the tide of events and of political thought gained strength in this country with the approach of the Second World War, Sheean joined the intellectuals in retreat. He slid from the socialist science of Marx and Lenin to the mysticism of Mahatma Gandhi. Let us leave him dozing and dreaming at the spinning wheel about the virtues of passive resistance to evil so long as he doesn't catch hold of any of us and try to pull us back with him.

It was a decisive step in the process of evolution, we pointed out, when the first creature acquired a backbone. There have been many relapses in the movement of history, especially in the world-shaking struggles of our own generation. Many people became frightened by the immensity of the tasks or crushed by adversity to the point of losing their moral and intellectual backbones and of losing sight of the direction of social evolution. This has happened in recent years to many more than Vincent Sheean in both labor and intellectual circles.

This "lost generation" has forgotten, if they ever learned, the supreme lesson of both world history and American history. This is that the forces making for the advancement of mankind have overcome the most formidable obstacles and have won out in the end. Otherwise, we should not be here to tell the tale or to help in making its next chapter.

Our animal ancestors progressed from the fish to the ape; our human ancestors have climbed upward from the ape to Republican President Eisenhower of the United States and conservative President Meany of the AFL-CIO. Along the way, they disposed of recalcitrant master classes, who, like the monopolists, refused to believe their sovereignty would ever end. Is it rational to think that men of their stripe are the ultimate representatives of the American nation and its labor movement or enduring shapers of the world's destiny, or that their reactionary policies and shortsighted outlook will prevail for decades?

The American people will bring forward in the future, as they have at critical times in the past, more audacious men and women with a vision of a new world in the making. These fighting leaders and leading fighters, guided by "the long view" of Marxism, will prove in practice that the socialist prospects of humanity, and of the American nation, are not so distant as they now appear.

About the author

GEORGE NOVACK (1905–1992) joined the communist movement in 1933, and remained a member and leader of the Socialist Workers Party until his death.

As national secretary of the American Committee for the Defense of Leon Trotsky, Novack helped organize the 1937 International Commission of Inquiry, headed by John Dewey, which investigated the Moscow frame-up trials. In the 1940s Novack was national secretary of the Civil Rights Defense Committee, which gathered support for leaders of the Socialist Workers Party and of the Midwest Teamsters strikes and organizing drives who were framed up and jailed during World War II under the witch-hunting Smith Act. He played a prominent role in numerous other civil liberties and civil rights battles over subsequent decades, including the landmark lawsuit against FBI spying and disruption won by the Socialist Workers Party in 1986. He was also active in defense of the Cuban revolution and against the war in Vietnam.

He lectured widely on Marxism at universities and public forums across the United States, Europe, Latin America, and the Pacific. Among the works he authored or edited are:

An Introduction to the Logic of Marxism • *Genocide against the Indians* • *The Origins of Materialism* • *Existentialism versus Marxism* • *Empiricism and Its Evolution* • *How Can the Jews Survive? A Socialist Answer to Zionism* • *The Marxist Theory of Alienation* • *Democracy and Revolution* • *Understanding History* • *Humanism and Socialism* • *Their Morals and Ours* • *The Revolutionary Potential of the Working Class* • *Pragmatism versus Marxism* • *America's Revolutionary Heritage* • *Polemics in Marxist Philosophy*

Also from Pathfinder

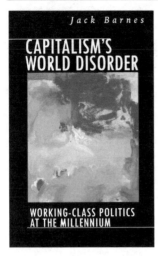

Capitalism's World Disorder

Working-Class Politics at the Millennium

JACK BARNES

The social devastation, financial panic, political turmoil, police brutality, and acts of imperialist aggression accelerating around us are not chaos. They are the product of lawful—and understandable—forces unleashed by capitalism. But the future the propertied classes have in store for us is not inevitable. It can be changed by the timely solidarity, courageous action, and united struggle of workers and farmers conscious of their power to transform the world. $23.95

Socialism: Utopian and Scientific

FREDERICK ENGELS

Modern socialism is not a doctrine, Engels explains, but a working-class movement growing out of the establishment of large-scale capitalist industry and its social consequences. $4.00

The Revolutionary Party

Its Role in the Struggle for Socialism

JAMES P. CANNON

The necessity of creating a leadership capable of carrying through to the end the struggle of working people to conquer power. $2.00

The Transitional Program for Socialist Revolution

LEON TROTSKY

Contains discussions between leaders of the U.S. Socialist Workers Party and exiled revolutionary Leon Trotsky in 1938. The product of these discussions, a program of immediate, democratic, and transitional demands, was adopted by the SWP later that year. This program for socialist revolution remains an irreplace-able component of a fighting guide for communist workers today. $23.95

Understanding History

Marxist Essays

GEORGE NOVACK

How did capitalism arise? Why and when did this exploitative system exhaust its once progressive role? Why is revolutionary change fundamental to human progress. $15.95

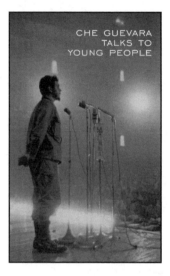

Che Guevara Talks to Young People

The legendary Argentine-born revolutionary challenges youth of Cuba and the world to work and become disciplined. To fearlessly join the front lines of struggles, small and large. To read and to study. To aspire to be revolutionary combatants. To politicize the organizations they are part of and in the process politicize themselves. To become a different kind of human being as they strive together with working people of all lands to transform the world. And, along this line of march, to renew and revel in the spontaneity and joy of being young. $14.95

Imperialism: The Highest Stage of Capitalism

V.I. LENIN

"I trust that this pamphlet will help the reader to understand the fundamental economic question, that of the economic essence of imperialism," Lenin wrote in 1917. "For unless this is studied, it will be impossible to understand and appraise modern war and modern politics." $3.95

By Any Means Necessary

MALCOLM X

Speeches tracing the evolution of Malcolm X's views on political alliances, women's rights, intermarriage, capitalism and socialism, and more. $15.95

Available from Pathfinder

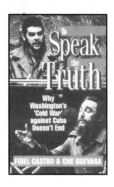

To Speak the Truth
Why Washington's 'Cold War' against Cuba
Doesn't End

FIDEL CASTRO AND CHE GUEVARA

In historic speeches before the United Nations and UN
bodies, Guevara and Castro address the workers of the
world, explaining why the U.S. government so hates the
example set by the socialist revolution in Cuba and why
Washington's effort to destroy it will fail. $16.95

The Origin of the Family, Private Property, and the State

FREDERICK ENGELS
INTRODUCTION BY EVELYN REED

How the emergence of class-divided society gave rise to
repressive state bodies and family structures that
protect the property of the ruling layers and enable
them to pass along wealth and privilege. Engels
discusses the consequences for working people of these
class institutions—from their original forms to their
modern versions. $17.95

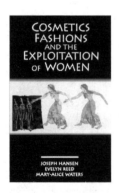

Cosmetics, Fashions, and the Exploitation of Women

JOSEPH HANSEN, EVELYN REED, AND
MARY-ALICE WATERS

How big business promotes cosmetics to generate
profits and perpetuate the inferior status of women. The
introduction by Waters explains how the entry of
millions of women into the workforce during and after
World War II irreversibly changed U.S. society and laid
the basis for a renewed rise of struggles for women's
equality. $12.95

Teamster Rebellion

FARRELL DOBBS

The 1934 strikes that built the industrial union movement in Minneapolis and
helped pave the way for the CIO, recounted by a central leader of that battle.
The first in a four-volume series on the class-struggle leadership of the strikes and
organizing drives that transformed the Teamsters union in much of the Midwest
into a fighting social movement and pointed the road toward independent labor
political action. $16.95

Write for a catalog. See addresses in front of booklet